P9-BYJ-996

Will We Miss Them?
ENDANGERED SPECIES

by Alexandra Wright

illustrated by Marshall Peck III

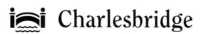 Charlesbridge

For Beth Mira Aimée Benjamin Huguette Ann Chris MHP Jr. — MHP III

Text and illustrations Copyright © 1992 by Charlesbridge
All rights reserved, including the right of reproduction in whole or in part in any form.
Charlesbridge and colophon are registered trademarks of Charlesbridge Publishing, Inc.
Library of Congress Catalog Card Number 91-73359
ISBN 0-88106-488-2 (softcover)
ISBN 0-88106-489-0 (reinforced for library use)
Published by Charlesbridge, 85 Main Street, Watertown, MA 02472 • (617) 926-0329
www.charlesbridge.com
Printed in Korea
(sc) 20 19 18 17 16
(hc) 10 9 8 7 6 5 4

Will We Miss Them?

This book is about some amazing animals that are disappearing from the Earth. Some are becoming scarce because poachers (people who hunt illegally) kill them for their horns, tusks, skins, or fur. Others are vanishing because they cannot compete with people for space, water, or food. Will we miss these animals? Can we help save them? The first step is to learn who they are.

Will we miss the bald eagle?

The bald eagle is not really bald. It is
called bald because from a distance you
can't see the white feathers on its head.

Bald eagles build huge nests — eight or nine feet wide.
When there are no big old trees in peaceful, quiet places,
bald eagles have no place to build their nests. Once, bald
eagles lived in every state except
Hawaii, but now they are
thriving only in the state
of Alaska and in parts
of Canada where
there are lots of big
trees.

These bald eagles are searching for their dinner. Bald eagles have better eyesight than almost all other creatures. They can spot small animals moving in a field a mile away!

Will we miss the African elephant?

African elephants are the largest creatures on land. Their babies weigh more than grown-up people do! The elephant's trunk is really an upper lip and nose. The muscles on the top of the trunk are very strong and can be used for pushing. The underside is much more delicate.

You will never see an elephant striking a blow with its trunk because that would hurt. The trunk is not used as a drinking straw, either. The elephant takes water up into its trunk and then squirts it into its mouth.

Elephants are endangered because of two problems — poachers and farmers. As more people try to farm the land, there is less space for the elephants. Also, poachers kill elephants for their valuable ivory tusks. You can help protect elephants by refusing to buy anything made of ivory.

Will we miss the blue whale?

The blue whale is the largest living creature on our planet. It can weigh more than thirty elephants! A newborn blue whale calf weighs 2,000 pounds and gains 200 pounds a day every day for the first year. If you gained weight at that rate, at your first birthday you'd weigh almost 300 pounds!

People once thought that whales were fish because whales live in the water. But whales are mammals that must breathe air through a blowhole, which is like a nostril on the top of a whale's head. For many years, people hunted whales for their meat and for their blubber, which was used to make oil for lamps and other things. Now that we have electricity for light and know how to pump oil from oil wells, there is no reason to kill whales.

Will we miss the panda?

The panda lives in only a few small areas of China, in places where plenty of bamboo grows. Pandas will eat small rodents and several kinds of plants, but their favorite food is bamboo. This panda may eat up to forty pounds of bamboo each day. For hours it happily chomps on bamboo shoots. Bamboo splinters don't bother the panda because its throat has a lining that protects it from splinters.

In this picture, the pandas look cute and cuddly, but they are actually quite big and have coarse fur. A full-grown panda may weigh 165 pounds or more.

Pandas have been hunted and have been unable to survive when the bamboo forests died or were cut down. China has passed laws to protect the panda, and pandas are now a worldwide symbol of conservation.

Will we miss the Galapagos tortoise?

The Galapagos tortoise lives only on the Galapagos Islands. When the first people arrived, there were so many tortoises that the people could not have walked across the islands without walking on tortoises! Unfortunately, when these explorers landed, rats left their ships. These rats ate the tortoise eggs.
The people made tortoise soup.
Today, few tortoises are left.

When a baby tortoise does grow up, it *really* grows up. The one in this picture weighs 600 pounds. Galapagos tortoises live longer than any other animal on Earth. If nothing harms this tortoise, it may live to be two hundred years old!

No one knows what it means, but these tortoises make a bellowing sound like a trumpet blast. A bellowing tortoise is so loud that you can hear it over a mile away!

Will we miss the mountain lion?

The North American mountain lion
is also called the puma, cougar, and panther.
People used to fear these big cats and killed
them whenever they were near.

East of the Mississippi River, few mountain
lions are left except for the Florida panther.
The Florida panther is one of the most secretive
animals. This big cat sometimes spends its days
in trees and usually hunts at night.

The cougar of Arizona and New Mexico is the largest unspotted cat in North and South America. It is over 8 feet long from the tip of its tail to its nose and weighs over 200 pounds. This huge cat can jump as high as a second story window. Wow, what a great jumper!

Will we miss the whooping crane?

As winter approaches, the whooping crane flies south to the salt marshes of the Texas Gulf Coast. Its 2,000 mile journey from Canada is full of dangers. It must avoid hungry wolves and coyotes, accidental shooting, power lines, and strong winds.

The whooping crane nearly became extinct. In 1941, only 21 of these large, white cranes were still alive. Then laws were passed to ban all shooting of whooping cranes and to protect their nesting grounds. These laws have helped to save the bird from extinction.

By 1990, people counted 150 whooping cranes, including full-grown birds and their cinnamon-colored babies.

Will we miss the grizzly bear?

Grizzlies like to live in places that make good farms, like open meadows and river valleys. This means that they often compete with people for space and food. Grizzlies eat almost anything — berries, leaves, small animals, fish, or even roots. Grizzlies who live on the West Coast enjoy feasting on salmon in the summer.

In winter, a grizzly finds a cave or a hollow log to use as a den for a long winter sleep. Kitten-sized cubs are born in the winter and are already bigger than a basketball when they leave the den with their mother in the spring. In the United States, except for Alaska, few grizzlies remain. The best place to see one is in the national parks, where they are protected.

Will we miss the manatee?

Manatees are air-breathing mammals that are related to elephants. Even though manatees are huge, they are playful and peaceful animals. They swim by moving their tails up and down and using their flippers to steer. In shallow water, manatees can "walk" on their flippers. Sometimes they even use their flippers to hug each other!

Manatees live in the warm waters of southern rivers. When they come to the surface to breathe, they are in danger. They are too slow to swim out of the way of motorboats. Many are killed when boats hit them. Others make the mistake of trying to live in the warm streams that come from power plants. If the power plants break down, the manatees catch cold and die unless they find another source of warm water.

Will we miss the muriqui?

Like a trained acrobat, a muriqui swings through the trees, using its tail, hands, and feet. Its tail is prehensile, which means it is used for grasping, just like a fifth hand. A muriqui can swing by its tail or even hang upside down by it.

The gap between these trees is too big for the baby muriqui to cross, so its mother is making a body bridge between the branches. Muriquis hardly ever come down out of the trees. They live only in the southeastern forest along the coast of Brazil. This area, unfortunately, is also where most of the people live.

As the forests are cut down, the muriquis are disappearing. Out of the thousands that used to live in Brazil, only a few hundred are left. There are so many people who care about the survival of the muriquis that this monkey is the symbol of conservation in Brazil, just as the panda is in China.

Will we miss the rhinoceros?

The name rhinoceros may sound kind of funny, but it means "nose horn." The horn on the rhino's nose grows . . . and grows — as much as 3 inches a year. The rhinoceros is the only animal that has a horn growing from its nose. Other animals have horns growing on the tops or sides of their heads. A mother rhinoceros uses her horn to protect her baby from lions, hyenas, and crocodiles.

There are five kinds of rhinos. Some have only one horn, others have two. But all rhinos have very poor eyesight and must drink water often. That makes them easy to kill. It is against the law to kill rhinos, but poachers still kill them for their horns, which are very valuable. There are now very few rhinos left, and most of them live in protected reserves.

Will we miss the mountain gorilla?

The mountain gorilla is the largest living primate. This gentle, shy creature is the only ape that likes to spend most of its time on the ground instead of in the trees. It eats seeds, fruit, nettles, wild celery, thistles, and other plants. With an opposable thumb like humans have, these apes can pick up the smallest seeds. Only a few hundred mountain gorillas are still alive. They live in a few small areas of central Africa, where they are studied and protected.

You might see a lowland gorilla in a zoo, but a mountain gorilla can only live if it is free. A group of mountain gorillas is led by a large, silverbacked male. He protects the group and leads it through the forest. Newborn babies weigh about 4½ pounds. Their mothers and aunts feed and carry them, and shelter them in a nest of branches at night. Just like people, their babies can't walk until they are about one year old.

Will we miss the crocodile?

The big toothy mouth of a crocodile is really amazing. It has about 100 sharp teeth. When one tooth falls out, a new one grows in very quickly, and new ones can grow in again 45 times! Even with all these teeth, this mother crocodile can be very gentle. After she makes a nest and lays her eggs, she watches carefully until the eggs hatch. Then she opens her mouth so her babies can climb in to get a ride down to the water.

The babies never finish growing up. They grow bigger every year of their lives. Imagine if people did that!

Some crocodiles are endangered because they are killed for their valuable skins and because they are dangerous neighbors. A crocodile lying in the sun to get warm can surprise you. Watch out! If disturbed, it can run as fast as a race horse for a short distance.

Blue Whale
Balaenoptera musculus

Grizzly Bear
Ursus horribilis

Whooping Crane
Grus americana

Bald Eagle
Haliaeetus leucocephalus

Grizzly Bear
Ursus horribilis

Bald Eagle
Haliaeetus leucocephalus

Mountain Lion
Felis concolor

Manatee
Trichechus manatus

Mountain Lion
Felis concolor

Whooping Crane
Grus americana

Orinoco Crocodile
Crocodylus intermedius

Manatee
Trichechus inunguis

Galapagos Tortoise
Geochelone elephantopus

Muriquis
Brachyteles arachnoides

Blue Whale
Balaenoptera musculus

Will we miss them?

Yes, we probably will. Each animal is part of a pattern that is woven into everyone's life.

But we don't have to miss them. We still have time to save these endangered animals. We can save them because, like the whooping crane, they are beautiful. We can save them because, like the grizzly bear, they are an important part of our heritage. We can save them for the most important reason of all — they are all part of the amazing balance of nature that makes life so wonderful.

Protection of wildlife is very important now because so many species are endangered. Millions of wild animals are killed every year to supply people with fur coats, souvenirs, and exotic pets. Special habitats such as salt marshes are destroyed by pollution. Rain forests are cut down for their wood and to make more space for farms, homes, and industry.

Blue Whale
Balaenoptera musculus

Giant Panda
Ailuropoda melanoleuca

Indian Elephant
Elephas maximus bengalensis

Indian Rhinoceros
Rhinoceros unicornis

Indian Gavial
Gavialis gangeticus

Nile Crocodile
Crocodylus niloticus

Saltwater Crocodile
Crocodylus porosus

African Elephant
Loxodonta africana

Sumatran Rhinoceros
Dicerorhinus sumatrensis

Manatee
Trichechus senegalensis

Javan Rhinoceros
Rhinoceros sondaicus

Mountain Gorilla
Gorilla gorilla beringei

Saltwater Crocodile
Crocodylus porosus

To help endangered species,
learn everything you can
about them, and tell other
people about them. Visit
the zoo and your local
library to find out about wild
animals in your area. No matter
where you live, you can do something. If
we all care, we can make our world a place
where people and animals can live together in harmony.

White Rhinoceros
Ceratotherium simum

Black Rhinoceros
Diceros bicornis

Blue Whale
Balaenoptera musculus